SHAPES

Circles

by Marybeth Lorbiecki

illustrated by Sharon Holm

Content Consultant: Paula J. Maida, Ph.D.
Department of Mathematics, Western Connecticut State University

magic wagon

visit us at
www.abdopublishing.com

Published by Magic Wagon, a division of the ABDO Publishing Group, 8000 West 78th Street, Edina, Minnesota, 55439.

Printed in the United States.

Text by Marybeth Lorbiecki
Illustrations by Sharon Holm
Edited by Patricia Stockland
Interior layout and design by Becky Daum
Cover design by Becky Daum

Library of Congress Cataloging-in-Publication Data

Lorbiecki, Marybeth.
Circles / Marybeth Lorbiecki ; illustrated by Sharon Holm.
p. cm. — (Shapes)
ISBN 978-1-60270-043-7
1. Circle—Juvenile literature. 2. Geometry—Juvenile literature. I. Holm, Sharon Lane, ill. II. Title.
QA484.L67 2008
516'.152—dc22

2007004695

Take a curve and swirl it round.

There you have a circle found.

Look around for this shape's look.

Look for circles in this book.

Find them in your ice cream bowl.

Spy one in the doughnut hole.

Circles form whole pizza pies,

open mouths, and open eyes.

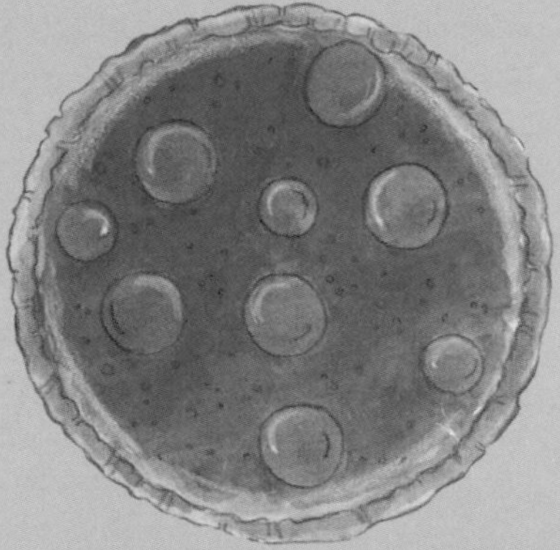

Spot the cookies, nice and sweet!

Fill the plate with circle treats.

In the yard, there is a loop.

The circle makes a hula-hoop.

See the clown with circles high.

Count the circles in the sky.

Now find the circle in the pool.

Jump in this circle to stay cool.

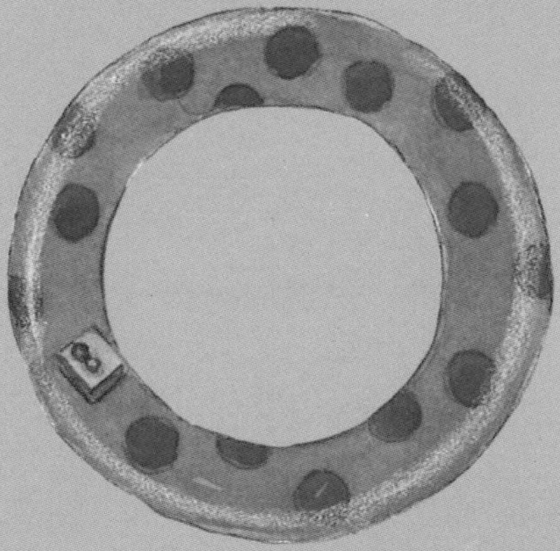

Sit under circles to block the sun.

Juggle circles for some fun.

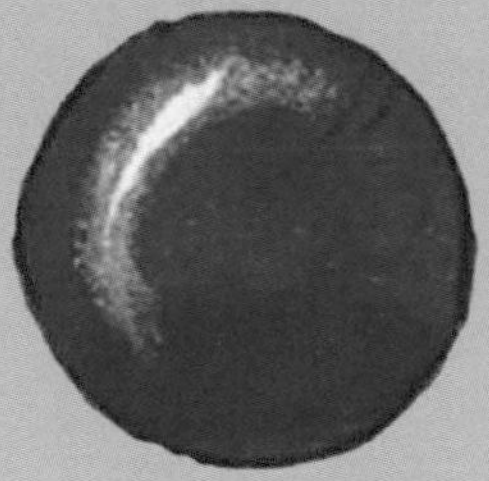

Frost the circles on top of this cake.

Now share the circles you have baked!

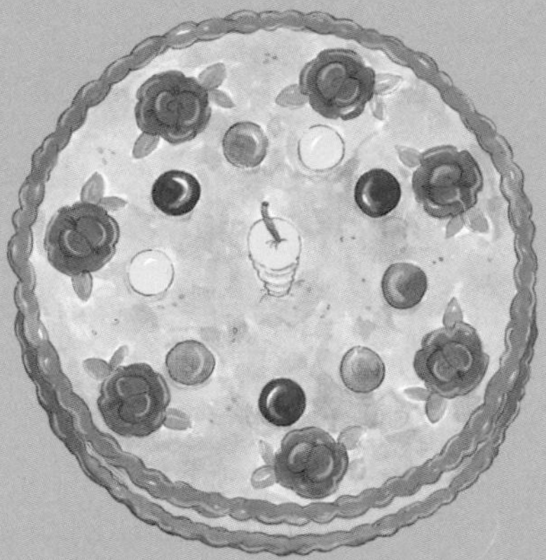

Circles aren't just in this book.

They're all around you. Take a look!

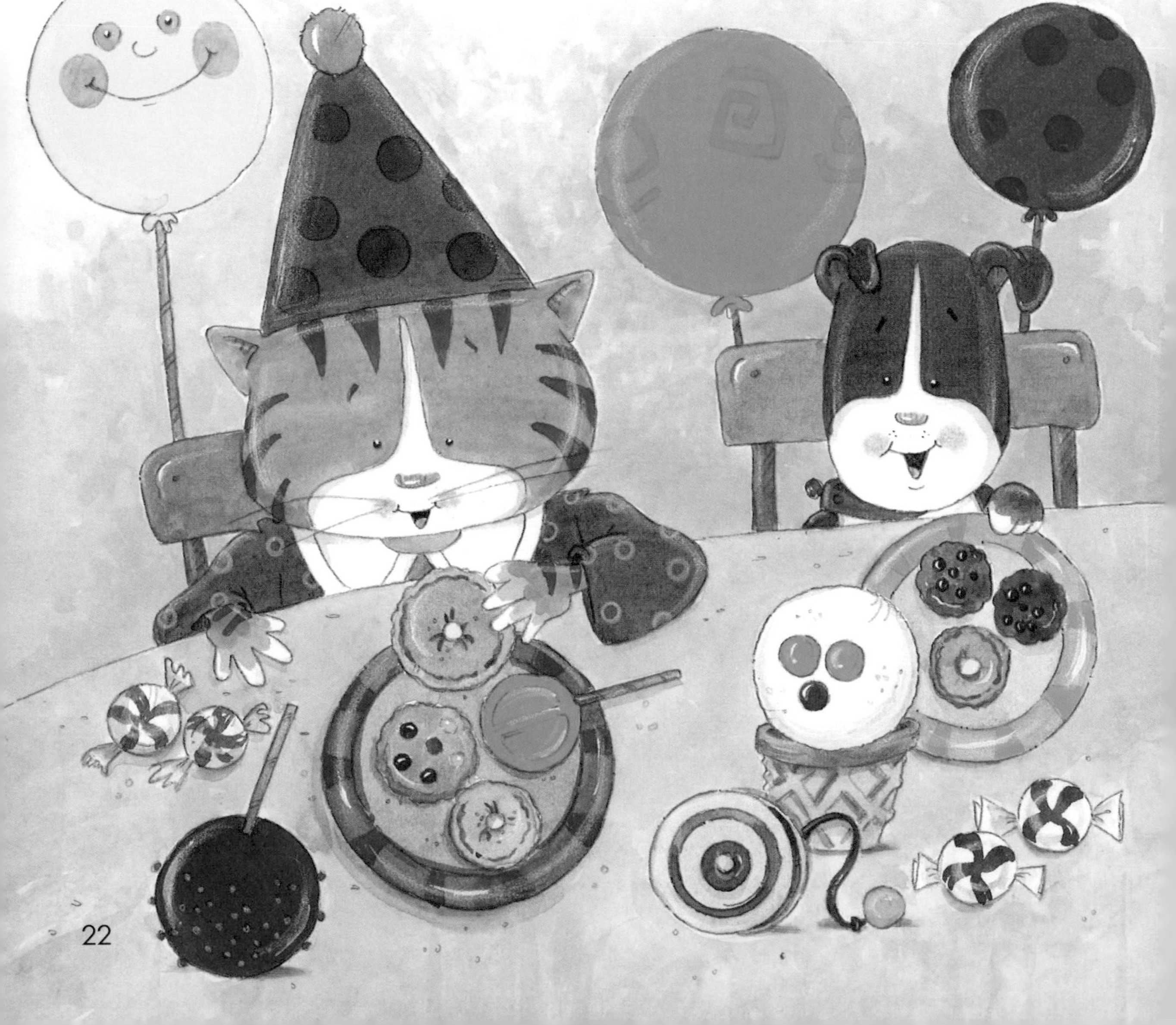

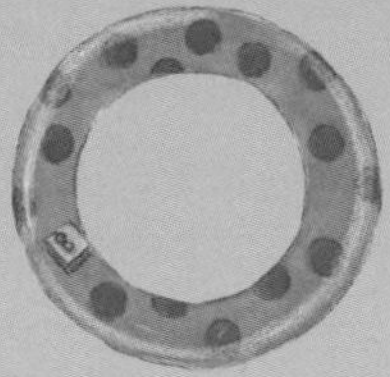

I Spy a Circle Game

Look around. Find a circle. Then say: "I spy a circle that is..." and name its color. Everyone has to guess what circle you see. Then it is someone else's turn to spy a circle. You can guess what it is.

Count the Circles Game

Pick a room in your home. Count how many circles you can find.

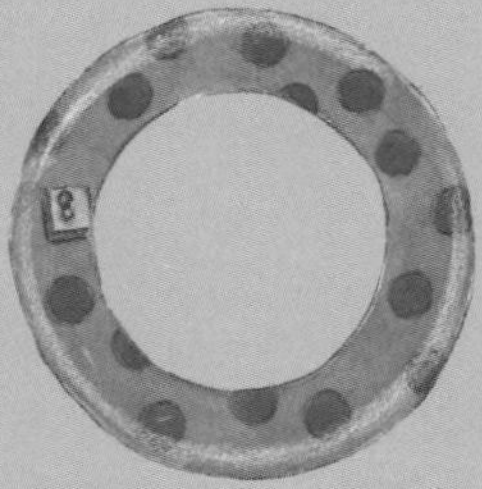

Words to Know

circle: a shape that is all round.

loop: a shape made by a curve.

round: something that has curved edges and has an equal distance from the center to any part of the edge.

shape: the form or look something has.